A Beginner's Guide to

Desert Survival Skills

Knowledge and Skills to Survive in the Desert

Prepping and Survival Books

Dueep Jyot Singh

Mendon Cottage Books

JD-Biz Publishing

Disclaimer

The information is this book is provided for informational purposes only. It is not intended to be used and medical advice or a substitute for proper medical treatment by a qualified health care provider. The information is believed to be accurate as presented based on research by the author.

The contents have not been evaluated by the U.S. Food and Drug Administration or any other Government or Health Organization and the contents in this book are not to be used to treat cure or prevent disease.

The author or publisher is not responsible for the use or safety of any diet, procedure or treatment mentioned in this book. The author or publisher is not responsible for errors or omissions that may exist.

Warning

The Book is for informational purposes only and before taking on any diet, treatment or medical procedure, it is recommended to consult with your primary health care provider.

Our books are available at

1. Amazon.com
2. Barnes and Noble
3. Itunes
4. Kobo
5. Smashwords
6. Google Play Books

Table of Contents

Introduction 4

Protecting Yourself in a Desert 6

Low Ground Versus High Ground 9

Common Sense Survival Tips 13

Car Breakdown in the Desert 15

Traveling in a Dust Storm Area 19

Protective Clothing 21

Desert Survival Kit... 24

    Food 24

    Why a Good Lighter?...25

    Trapping Food in the Desert 29

    Extremely easy Hopi bird snare 30

    Making Slipknots 30

    Making a Slingshot 30

Conclusion 33

Author Bio.. 34

Publisher.. 44

Introduction

I remember seeing Lost in the Desert as a child, and there are just some scenes which I remember. The father of a child lost in the desert believes that his child has survived a plane crash. So he gets millions of leaflets printed and airdropped all over the desert, with survival tips to his son, reassuring him that his father will find him, and all he has to do is survive.

Dirkie and his dog survived – this movie -made by Jamie Uys who then produced the hugely successful The Gods Must Be Crazy – is based on a true story. So the first point is, you need to have a will to survive.

Movies and reality apart, how is it possible for people to survive in the desert, especially in adverse weather conditions for centuries? How is it that people in the Kalahari, in the Sahara or in the Thar desert do not mind living out their lives in such bleak and harsh conditions?

Fortunately, a majority of our 21st century world is still green and does not consist of miles and miles of land with no water and no food in sight. Well there is a slight lack of knowledge here. There is food and water in the desert. It depends on us to know how to get it. This book is going to give you information, especially useful tips and techniques, on how to preserve you and survive in desert conditions, especially when you are on limited food and water supplies.

Protecting Yourself in a Desert

I enjoy Clive Cussler books, because his rough and tough characters Pitt and Giordino use amazingly effective tips and techniques to survive adverse conditions, including getting lost in the desert.

I remember when I was about eight years old, and found myself in the middle of a desert storm. I had been brought up in a mountainous area, and coming for a holiday in a desert area was good for short stretches, but definitely not amusing to a person who was used to plenty of greenery, water and food in abundance. But this was another adventurous way of life.

So this dust storm – which is normally called a Khamsin in Egypt – and terrible in its intensity blew up, when our adventure trainer and mentor father had taken his two kids in the desert to show us that particular terrain on the surface of the earth.

Now the sandstorms are unpredictable. You cannot know that they are going to strike an area, because you do not get any warning. Visibility is going to be nil, in less than a minute.

He immediately told us to wrap our faces up with pieces of cloth, so that our nostrils did not get clogged with particles of dust. A scarf, a handkerchief or anything through which you can breathe easily can be used. We did not have petroleum jelly with us, otherwise he would have asked us to apply that in the inside of our nostrils, so that that portion did not dry up. But if you are going out in the desert, you are going to have some of this moisturizing petroleum jelly with you, to protect your skin, are not you. So apply it liberally.

After that, he told us to wrap our heads and ears. We were going to protect our eyes by placing our arms over them. Sunglasses do not work here, because the particles of sand are going to pit the surface of the glass, because the wind is going to blow with extreme force. There are air tight goggles available, but in their paucity, use your arms.

After that, he told us – look for the nearest hill and climb it. We looked around and there were no hills and sand dunes around. So what did we do under such circumstances? It was just plain ground.

In worst come worst circumstances, we would lie down on the ground and protect our bodies with a backpack or with our arms.

We did not have backpacks. But we had protective clothes on which covered our bodies from head to foot.

Saw that picture above of that woman lost in the desert?

She is definitely dehydrated. She is foolish enough not to wear a head covering or to wear protective clothing protecting her skin from the sun and the sand. Not only she going to get dreadfully sunburnt, but she is losing moisture fast. So, first thing, fashionable sportswear and being fashionably suntanned takes a back seat when you are in a desert. Use some common sense.

The sun and the dry air is going to be your most powerful enemy. So protect yourself from the sun by covering yourself up from head to toe.

Low Ground Versus High Ground

You are always going to find some area in the desert, you can get rock outcroppings. Try to get shelter under them during the day.

Do you lie under a sand dune in a sandstorm? No way.

For millenniums, natives know all about how to make a hole in the sand and bury them, waiting out the storm, but we were taking no chances. We had definitely no intention of lying down and being buried on plain ground. Who knew how long the Khamsin would blow? And we were definitely not ready and willing to be buried alive under piles of sand with no one knowing where to dig to rescue us after the storm had blown over.

The whole shape and map of a desert changes the moment a sandstorm blows up. Dunes lift themselves and shift to another location in the desert. However, the largest concentration of dust and dry sand is going to bounce away closest to the ground, swirling in the wind. So when you are on higher ground, there is less chance of you being buried under this intense gale of sand.

You have to be very careful here. If the desert storm is accompanied by lightning, **do not** climb up on a higher level. Also, if there is plenty of debris flying, do not climb up on the hill, or on the dune. You are going to get knocked out under such circumstances.

When the Desert Storm is accompanied by lightning, well then, you need to take shelter on the low ground.

Do not dive for the nearest ditch or in a place where you know water has been flowing. Any water coming down as rain in the desert area normally dries up before it reaches the dry, dusty surface, but sometimes, when storm clouds gather, these ditches are going to be filled up with water from other low-lying areas in the desert. You can consider them to be flash floods.

So if you are in a Wadi, arroyo, ditch, scramble out of it as soon as possible.

We had camels, so he immediately made us get off our camels and our guide made them sit down. After that we pressed ourselves to the Leeward side of the camel. This was the side protected against the wind. These camels did not mind the Desert Storms, because after all they were born and brought up in the desert.

But we had protection. We had a solid barrier of the camel against the wind. Our guide had told us not to hide under a sand dune, because as I said before, huge piles of sand shifted in the wind. And many travelers found themselves buried alive in the desert, just because they thought to protect themselves from the wind by placing themselves on the leeward of a sand dune.

A camel has adapted itself to survive in the desert. So have a number of little animals like scorpions, snakes, lizards, insects, deer, and birds.

If you do not have a camel around to protect you from unidentified and identified flying objects, look for a solid land form, especially a rock. Try to wriggle as far as possible as you can under the shelter of the rock. I still remember the stinging blows of those terrible tiny dust particles battering my face, because I took a bit too long to cover it.

Common Sense Survival Tips

Do not try to out run a storm, when you are on foot

Desert nomads know that it is extremely foolish to think of running out a storm. The wall of sand moves fast. So stay where you are and stay put. Moving through storms, as shown in the movies is one of the most idiotic things that you can do. Wait for the storm to blow itself out before you decide to move to another location.

If you are lucky to have shelter in the shape of four walls and a roof, get in before the storm strikes, and shut all the doors and windows. Wait out this sandstorm before trying to move out.

I remember one survival rule, which may not work here, but which I am putting in for general knowledge, if you find yourself caught in a fog. This has been taken from Maurice Walsh's, the Small Dark Man.

"If the mist comes down on you at the cairn, sit on a stone and wait; and if a mist smothers you across the flat, stick your ash plant walking stick in the peat. And if you have the time, put up a stone 10 feet away on the line you are going and keep your feet between the stone and the stick. Something calls you to move and if you wander, the mist will hang about you. Bide your place and the mist will move up before the wind is half an hour or less, and then you will have clear bit of air. You can move off your stone then. "

This book was published in 1932. Good sense of the ages, being used effectively.

I still think some of these survival tips, which also include a round pebble in your mouth, so that you do not suffer from dryness due to thirst to be very practical and sensible.

If you are in a group, and somebody decides to go wandering off in the desert in order to get help, squash his enthusiasm. He is just asking to commit suicide. Survival tactics do not include food hardy behavior which somebody considers to be heroic. There is nothing heroic about being lost in a desert.

Car Breakdown in the Desert

When your car breaks down right in the middle of a desert area when you are stranded on a road leading to nowhere, what do you do next? Do you get out, like the driver of this car and begin to wait for rescue? Depends on the circumstances. If somebody knows the direction in which you are going, just stay there. The GPS, if you are being tracked by satellite is going to help you get back to your destination safe and sound.

Stay put and put the blame where it is due. On you.

A breakdown definitely is not going to happen with cars which have been well-maintained and which are made especially for desert use, however, often this idiotic submission team is being used by escapist novel publishers.

And then the romantic Sheik comes riding upon his black charger, to rescue the aristocratic beautiful bubblehead female. E.M.Hull and P.C.Wren has much to answer for. In real life, that is not going to happen. Bubblehead will need to use some judgment and common sense in order to survive.

If you are in a car, try to out run the storm, is it is still far away. Look for detours and alternate routes. This was the advice given to me by a person who lives in the desert area, but I know all about rash drivers finding themselves in a pileup, because they are more bothered about out running the storm, than driving sensibly. Especially when you are in the middle of it, and the visibility is zero.

Of course, the thought of out running a storm on foot is an idea only bubbleheads and dimwits consider even remotely feasible. Cannot be done. Should not be done.

If the storm is more than 75 km/h, it is going to catch up with you. So use a little bit of initiative and start preparing to wait out the storm.

Park your car in a safe place, where your car is going to be sheltered. If you are driving, and on the road without any shelter, and the storm comes up suddenly, drive to the side of the road and get off the freeway. Turn off your headlights, turn signals and brake lights. Shut your doors and windows. Set a parking brake.

If you have not managed to turn off the highway, and are still driving, switch on your headlights and start sounding your horn. Creep on the road slowly. With your guiding centerline, keep driving until you reach the nearest spot where you can turn off the highway. Park your car there.

Turning all the lights off means that nobody is using your rear lights as a guiding light. I remember getting caught in a fog when coming down the mountain with my cousin driving. There were eight of us in the car and the road was a mountainous road, with zero visibility. There was absolutely no place on that narrow road, on which anybody could Park, because there was no proper space.

So here we were, with night coming on, all of us five adults rather worried, but trying not to show it because we had three children with us. So, first rule when you are traveling with children, let them think that you have everything under control.

My cousin decided that he would take a chance and he kept waiting till a really expensive car came down that road. That driver was taking a chance too. My cousin made sure that we were about 10 feet away from him, and so we began crawling down that mountain guided by the rear lights of the car in front. About half way down, when we came out of the fog, I asked my cousin why he took that chance.

His answer was – "That driver spent half a million on that particular car brand. He was definitely going to take extreme care to make sure that nothing happened to it. So I chose him as a guide."

You may not have a guiding car worth half 1 million in front of you. So it is better not to take any chances. Pull over to the nearest plain area away from road traffic, where nothing can hit you front or rear. Sitting on the side of the road with your lights on means that possibly some car is using the rear lights as a guiding light and it is going to collide with your rear bumper.

My suggestion is do not drive when you are in the middle of a sandstorm. Just wait it out. Dimwitted heroines decide to drive through the storm and end up in the hospital. Their beautiful faces are definitely unmarked in that terrible accident. Naturally, they have collided with the Rolls-Royce of a billionaire who decides that he is going to take on the responsibility of paying their hospital bills and then marrying them on page 186.

In real life if you meet with an accident, you are going to have the headache of getting your medical insurance company to pay for the bills. You may also end up badly hurt, physically, mentally, emotionally and psychologically.

You need to turn off all the air vents, which allow air to pass in. You would not want the inside of your car to be covered with dust, would you.

Traveling in a Dust Storm Area

Traveling in an area which is vulnerable to dust storms, especially in the desert should be done only when it is absolutely necessary. The storm warnings for possible dust storms are broadcast very often over the local and national radio and TV so listen to them. The storms are more common in the summertime and especially in known atmospheric conditions. Meteorologists through experience, get to know when these disturbances are going to take place. So listen to them.

In such cases, just do not go out of your house, unless absolutely necessary. I was reading a manuscript submitted to me by one of my writers in which the heroine decides to travel in a desert area, even though a dust storm was predicted. That is because the hero was a desert Prince. The critic in me said, Oh ho hum, how predictable and what a stupid female, she is. The publisher in me said, but then these books sell. So, as the submission guidelines have already been laid out by The Powers That Be, I have to say yes to this idiotic manuscript. I knew what would happen next. She would be rescued by the desert Prince.

If I was around her in real life, I would tell her that I did not think much about her IQ, especially when she was traveling in dry and hot conditions. Besides taking her car out into the desert, without bothering much about water, clothing, food, fuel and other forms of physical protection was just asking for trouble.

But then the writer knew that her tall dark handsome man – naturally Uber rich with European and American bloodlines so his family would allow him to marry bubble head – knight on a black charger would come riding by in just 10 minutes, before she got a chance to panic. And so the story meandered on.

Again, like I said, if you have to travel in a desert area, be prepared for the worst. A storm can occur anytime and is going to occur.

Protective Clothing

Nomads living in the desert area know how to survive in such harsh conditions, because they do not expose their body to the sun and the heat.

And that is why, their traditional robes cover every part of their body. I asked a friend of mine Yasmina, who just happens to be a Bedu- how her ancestors managed to live in the hot desert, if their clothes happened to be made of goat, camel and sheep wool. That was because I associated wool with warmth.

She told me that the original basic dress called a tob was and is made of cotton and was ankle length. Woolen tobs were spun in areas, where sheep and goat were plentiful. Sometimes, wool was the only material available with which they could spin their tobs.

This sensible clothing keeps this Bedu- Bedoin- cool in a hot, dry, arid atmosphere.

The loose fitting tunics allowed air to circulate throughout the body, and keep the body temperature regulated in times of heat and cold. That is because the desert temperature falls very sharply at night. Also, the cotton prevented the body from getting dehydrated. The sweat did not evaporate so quickly when the body was clothed in cotton, and the wearer went out in the hot sun.

People going out in the desert would always wear a headgear in the shape of kafiya-a square scarf which was fastened with a camel wool rope. This scarf could be unwrapped and opened up really easily to cover the head and the face the moment a dust storm came up.

So if you are going out in the desert wearing a sleeveless polyester T-shirt, you are just asking to be badly dehydrated.

If you do not have a long ankle length cotton tob, – wear clothes with long cotton sleeves and cotton khakis or loose fitting trousers. Also make sure that you are wearing sensible shoes and socks. Any clown who goes out in the desert wearing tight fitting shoes should have a keeper along of him. Remember that going out in the desert means that it is possible that you will have to walk over large areas of dry land.

Desert Survival Kit

Food

Many desert cacti species are edible.

I was reading a number of my favorite Westerns researching on just one point. All right, so these cowboys were having dinner in the desert. What did they eat and drink? I noticed that all these cowboys ate beans and meat and drank coffee. And here I was under the impression that they drank beer or whiskey ever so often even when cattle herding. After a bit of research I found out that this beer drinking was restricted only when they came to town and the job was done. They never drank any strong drink with alcoholic content when they were on duty, especially in the desert.

So I began to think – why coffee or later on, tomato juice in the late 19th century, when canned goods became readily available? Why not tins of beer? And then the light of logic clicked. The alcoholic content was extremely dehydrating. So here you are in the hot sun, drinking beer? Naturally, your body will need to eliminate liquids after a while. This precious fluid eliminated because you drank a substance which made your body get rid of liquid is going to weaken your body.

Experienced cowboys could not afford to take such chances of their health failing in the desert. The thin line between life and death at that time in that particular territory was already narrow enough without you stacking your cards *against* you.

So remember, if you are going out in the desert, leave your bottles of whiskey and beer behind. If you cannot do without them, what makes you think your journey is going to be successful across the desert, when you are going adventuring with potentially hazardous to your health items in your desert vehicle's icebox?

So remember to have plenty of water around. Always have a desert survival box in your vehicle, if you are driving. This is going to consist of an air filter mask, or if not that petroleum jelly as a last resort, goggles, a blanket or a sleeping bag for sleeping in a cold temperature at night, and of course apart from your desert survival knife, – try Victorinox or Swiss Army knives on eBay – you need to have a lighter and lighter fluid.

Why a Good Lighter?

I got into the habit of keeping a cigarette lighter in my purse, – even though our religion prevents tobacco use in any shape and form and I am not a smoker –, because I found that extremely useful. A lighter could be used to

---

light a fire, and take the place of a torch. It could be used as a protective weapon, especially against animals in the dark.

Also, man is subconsciously assured when he has fire around him. He is genetically programmed in this manner. So when he knows that he has the means to light a fire with which to keep him warm and to cook his food, when it is cold, wet and harsh weather outside his shelter, nothing can be so bad.

Try this psychological experiment. Go out in the rain on a dark night without a Macintosh. You are soon going to find yourself soaking wet and miserable. Look for shelter under a rock, and wait out the rain. Your mind is immediately going to start feeling low because it is naturally geared to feel blue during inclement weather. Take out your lighter. Click it. Naturally, your lighter has to be a good quality lighter, so that it lights up at the first instance itself.

The moment you see that fire, you are subconsciously and consciously going to feel more cheerful. Been there, seen that, proven that. It means that you can make a fire, you are not quite so helpless, can see in the dark with that little bit of light, and all the gremlins are at bay.

Try Zippo. These lighters are windproof and stay lit in harsh weather. Their prices start at USD12.95, but you can get them at lower prices on eBay. Backpackers, especially those caught in cold weather cannot do without them.

Well, I do not have a Zippo, but have a Chinese model, which frankly I have not tried out in cold, rainy weather. But it clicks on the moment I press the lever. I do not have to bother about Zippo's flint and spark mechanism.

This is what I have. But it works, each time every time. Good for keeping in your purse or in your pocket with easy access.

That reminds me of an old chestnut. A European explorer found himself captured by a native tribe and decided to show them some miracles. So he took out his lighter and said, "See how powerful I am. I have the power of fire in my hands. "And he clicked the lighter on. And the wavering yellow flame lit up all their astonished faces.

The explorer immediately waited for them to let him go because he was such a powerful being. Instead, one tribal member said to the other pensively, "The white man really can do miracles. That is the first time I saw a lighter light up when it was clicked just once."

Well, I think a reliable lighter should do just that, instead of you going click, click, click, exasperatedly while shivering away in the cold.

The bushmen in the Kalahari deserts and the aborigines of the Australian deserts know all about the value of the tubers, which are an excellent water storage source. You may want to see that amazing movie – The Gods Must Be Crazy to see them collecting water on leaves laid out in the previous evening and drinking it.

This is, of course, going to be done before the sun comes up, because all the dew disappears really fast, as soon as the sun rays hit the surface of the Kalahari.

This URL is going to give you amazing tips about finding edible foods in the desert.

http://www.desertusa.com/desert-activity/desert-food-hunting.html

In the holy Bible, it has been said that God fed the Israelites for 40 years with birds and manna.

Birds, rodents, animals, reptiles and other living creatures in the desert are all good sources of protein to help you survive.

If you are shocked at the mere thought of having to eat snakes, just imagine you are eating chicken. Yes, I have eaten snake, thinking it to be chicken. I could not notice any difference except the snake was softer and more delicious when roasted over a fire.

But that was of course after the head was chopped off, so there was no question of my eating a possibly poisonous snake. It was after we had appreciated that desert meal made up of nuts, berries, herbs and snake that we got to know that we were eating what the civilized world calls weeds to be destroyed by pesticides.

Learn to recognize the plants you can eat. Go out in the desert with an experienced guide, who can tell you all about eating the pulp of a cactus – excellent store of water – and the pads .

I did not know that we could eat all the parts of a dandelion. Uncooked leaves can be eaten in a salad. You can boil the leaves as a vegetable, especially in the spring. The roots need to be boiled for 30 minutes before eating, and are best eaten in the autumn/fall.

And that is why I wonder why so many traditional recipes, which used supposed weeds like a dandelion have gone out of common knowledge.

In her popular book Girl of the Limberlost, the mother of the heroine talks of feeding the convalescent hero with bacon and dandelion. I am sure she must have used fresh green dandelion leaves along with other herbs cooked with home cured bacon. Mmmmm, that sounds appetizing!

http://www.bio.brandeis.edu/fieldbio/Edible_plants/LetsEat_home.html

This site is extremely educational and interesting, because it gave me lots of information on edible plants.

Trapping Food in the Desert

This is a very broad-based topic, because it is going to depend on the materials that you have around you. Trapping food can only be done by an experienced person, who has got some training from a mentor who knows all about surviving in the desert.

However, you may like to look at all the tips and techniques given for trapping food on this amazing URL.

http://www.wilderness-survival.net/food-2.php

Extremely easy Hopi bird snare

https://www.youtube.com/watch?v=89bRQIyb93Q

When I was looking through this video, my first thought was, well, okay, I have made a noose. But how does the bird get caught in it?

That is because the knot is going to be a slipknot.

Making Slipknots

Slipknots are the first basic knots in knitting and crocheting, so once you know how to make these knots, remember to make all your snares with this knot.

https://www.youtube.com/watch?v=AqcPWw8YtfU

Making a Slingshot

This is an excellent tutorial on how to make a slingshot.

https://www.youtube.com/watch?v=eOuvLx_qU1o

But naturally your immediate reaction is going to be – where am I going to find a Y-shaped willow branch in a desert. Actually, this slingshot was made as a practice to see whether I could make this weapon. I did not have dental floss, so I used hundred percent nylon fishing yarn, which is equally strong.

http://www.artofmanliness.com/2012/05/14/diy-weekend-project-how-to-make-a-slingshot/

This is also very instructional.

When I was a child, we did not have latex surgical tubing around. So I asked my jungle bred friends how they got the material for the sides of the catapult and they said matter-of-factly, "animal intestines and dried muscle sinews." In fact, we used those intestines to make the bow strings for our bows.

I was not very good with bows and arrows, though all our Carrom and chessboard "Men" went for a six at 20 paces when I was around with my air gun. Father was definitely very annoyed when he had to buy these men again and again for our carom board and chessboard.

How could we have lost all of them?

They were not lost. Their remains were just interred with care under the nearest rose bush.

Till one day, he saw me potting them , and confiscated the air gun. Could not I hunt birdies and beasties? What was the fun in potting wooden carrom men and plastic chessboard men?

For me, it was what was the fun in potting birdies and beasties? I was not hungry.

He being an instinctive hunter did not understand that one did not need to make animals and birds a target, the moment you saw them. Besides, tiny targets were more of a challenge.

Jest call me Wild Bill Hiccup and when you say that,smile, podner.

Naturally, we did not have dental floss or nylon thread around at that time and the sinews were tied to the wood with others sinews and vines. Best natural weapons.

Remember that primitive man has been using dried muscles and sinews to make weapons down the ages. So if you are in the desert and have managed to trap a large animal, do not throw away the intestines. Allow them to dry. You can then remove the sinews and plait them to make a thick cord.

This book is, of course, a beginner's level book. Making weapons with sinews is advanced technology, done under the guidance of professionals. You may want to ask any experienced desert survival guide to teach you how to make weapons. And once they are made, practice!

Conclusion

I hope this beginner's guide to survival skills – desert survival has given you plenty of information on how to survive, especially when you find yourself in the desert. Most of these tips are common sense tips, but we do not take them into account. That is because most of us do not bother tapping into our survival instincts which have been inherited down the ages.

We would rather go by modern preconceived thoughts, which have been instilled in us by a tame conventional and thoroughly domesticated 21st-century civilization and society.

That is why the idea of living off the land, by eating insects, snakes, plants, herbs, seeds, trapped birds and raw, if we cannot build a fire is something which will make a majority of us shudder.

But consider you to be in a disaster situation. You know help is going to take a longish while to reach you. So you need to use your own intelligence and basic skills in order to survive till help arrives.

This book is giving you basics about survival in the desert. So read them, try them out, and gain assurance that you are going to manage to survive in the desert – when and if necessary.

Once you find the will to survive in your mind and spirit, half of the battle is won.

Live Long and Prosper.

Author Bio

Dueep Jyot Singh is a Management and IT Professional who managed to gather Postgraduate qualifications in Management and English and Degrees in Science, French and Education while pursuing different enjoyable career options like being an hospital administrator, IT,SEO and HRD Database Manager/ trainer, movie , radio and TV scriptwriter, theatre artiste and public speaker, lecturer in French, Marketing and Advertising, ex-Editor of Hearts On Fire (now known as Solstice) Books Missouri USA, advice columnist and cartoonist, publisher and Aviation School trainer, ex-moderator on Medico.in, banker, student councilor ,travelogue writer … among other things!

One fine morning, she decided that she had enough of killing herself by Degrees and went back to her first love -- writing. It's more enjoyable! She already has 48 published academic and 14 fiction- in- different- genre books under her belt.

When she is not designing websites or making Graphic design illustrations for clients , she is browsing through old bookshops hunting for treasures, of which she has an enviable collection – including R.L. Stevenson, O.Henry, Dornford Yates, Maurice Walsh, De Maupassant, Victor Hugo, Sapper, C.N. Williamson, "Bartimeus" and the crown of her collection- Dickens "The Old Curiosity Shop," and so on… Just call her "Renaissance Woman" - collecting herbal remedies, acting like Universal Helping Hand/Agony Aunt, or escaping to her dear mountains for a bit of exploring, collecting herbs and plants, and trekking.

Check out some of the other JD-Biz Publishing books

Gardening Series on Amazon

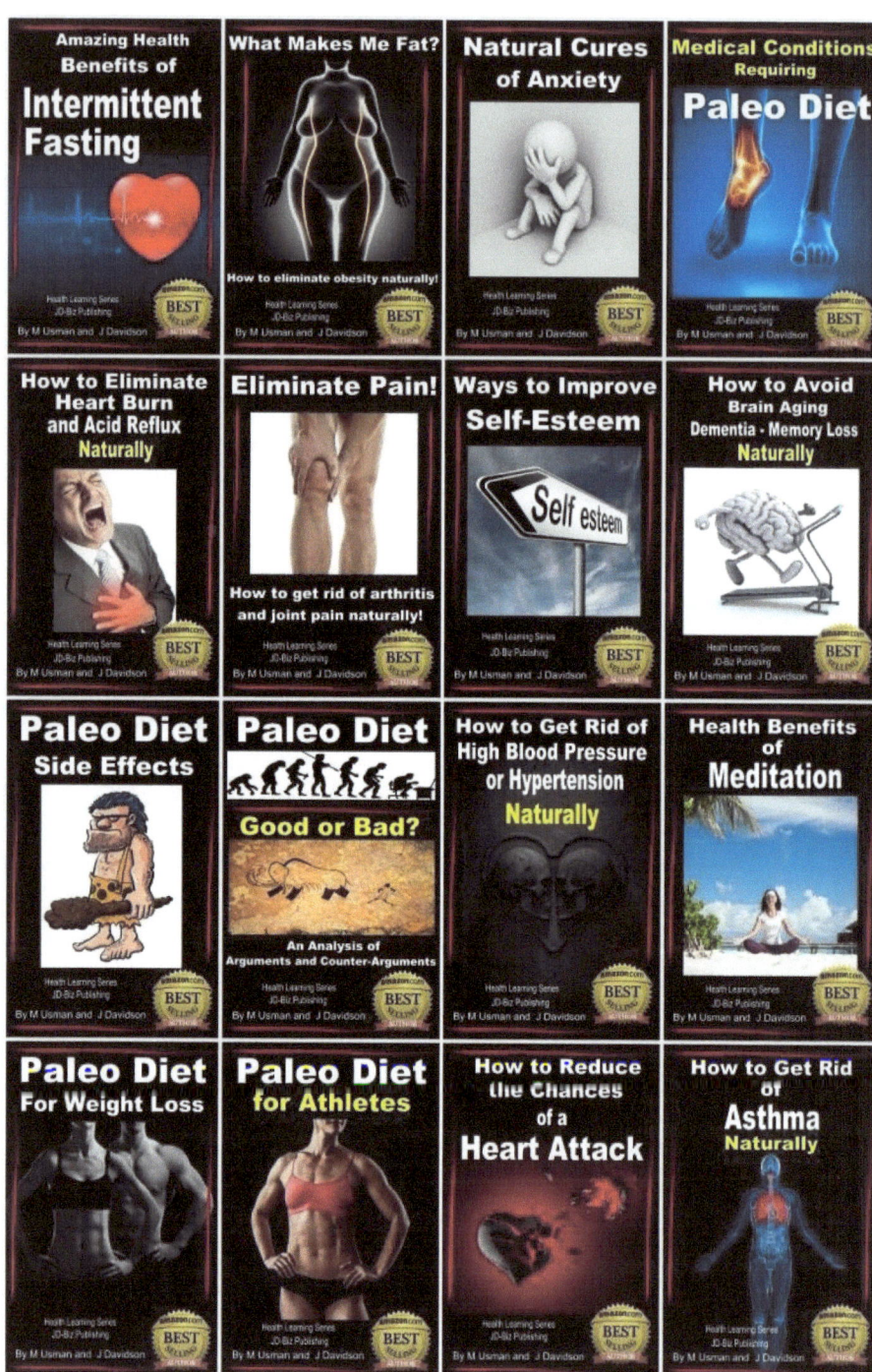

Amazing Animal Book Series

Learn To Draw Series

How to Build and Plan Books

Entrepreneur Book Series

Our books are available at

1. Amazon.com

2. Barnes and Noble

3. Itunes

4. Kobo

5. Smashwords

6. Google Play Books

Download Free Books!

http://MendonCottageBooks.com

Publisher

JD-Biz Corp

P O Box 374

Mendon, Utah 84325

http://www.jd-biz.com/

Mendon Cottage Books

P O Box 374, Mendon Utah 84325